MARRIED TO MARKETING
A RELATIONSHIP GUIDE TO BUSINESS

B. ZACHARY BENNETT

chantelar
PUBLISHING

Dedication

This book is dedicated to small business, entrepreneurs, growing companies, and those seeking to maintain success. I hope you find some value and wisdom herein. May we continue to walk together in the belief that knowledge is power and that an informed business is a better business.

Author Note

Though I used several illustrations throughout this book to make points of clarification and explanation, I have extreme admiration, respect, and appreciation for all of the business mentioned. Starting and operating a business takes courage, tenacity, and vision. All business owners should be held in high regard.

All companies, names, logos, histories, movies, packaging, promotions, and other works mentioned, shown, or described within this book are copyrighted by their respective creators.

CONTENTS

Foreword

by Jennifer Bennett

"I now pronounce you - husband and wife," says an older, cherub-faced man in a ponytail with a ukulele tucked under one arm. The beach was perfect that day in Maui and the sand warm under our toes. This moment was a long time coming... many would argue a lifetime in the making. In the age-old debate of which came first, "Marketing or the Marriage", I would have to answer Marketing. Our marriage was forged upon this bedrock of what we do.

Professionally, I have been Zachary's right-hand (wo)man at Reformation Productions since 2012. I am a Graphic Designer by trade and have been in this industry for about 15 years. Sure, Zachary has more experience, but I will continue to attribute that to the age gap between us (ha ha). As Art Director of the agency, I dabble in every aspect of client relations and creative production. My job seesaws between creative designer and genius-wrangler on a daily basis. In other words – I make things "pretty" and I translate "Zachary" for the agency's clients. From concept and research to strategy and development, Zachary and I live and breathe for the clients and the work that the agency can do for them. In the Marketing comic book I imagine in my head, Zachary and I are a Dynamic Duo... minus all the spandex.

Transitioning from professional to personal took time for us. It took dates out to Chattanooga, Tennessee and long rides together on the back of a Harley-Davidson motorcycle through the winding roads of the North Georgia Mountains. It even took a trip to Graceland just to try a peanut butter, banana and bacon sandwich. A thousand questions were asked and answered between the two of us. Desire was stoked, trust was built, and then a decision was made that would bond us together forever on the warm shoulder of Ironwoods Beach.

Now, every Saturday morning, we shuffle our way to the coffee pot then sit at the kitchen table and talk about something that will always eventually dissolve into commentary on marketing or branding. We talk about how things are being portrayed in the media or whether we've heard anything about the new restaurant in our area. We talk about business and the businesses that we knew growing up - the ones that have survived, thrived, and the ones that have died. Seeing the world through the lens of Marketing is every day to us. When we are out driving around, we see billboards and talk about them. We both get that heavy feeling when we see a newly emptied storefront because we know another business has probably folded. It bothers me greatly, and I know it drives Zachary nuts.

Zachary has dedicated his career to growing businesses. Having worked closely with many Fortune 500 brands as well as newer, smaller companies, he has seen the common mistakes that businesses make that threaten their sustainability. He works to provide education and suggestions to help save struggling businesses and build strong foundations for entrepreneurs so that they are properly prepared for success.

Of all the partnerships that a business owner can have, there is none more important than the one he has with his customer. The success of your company is a direct reflection of that relationship, so take the time to cultivate it. Zachary believes that taking the time to learn and "woo" your potential customer will provide a stronger more fruitful union – in much the same way you would seek out a romantic relationship.

He has always had a counselor's spirit and does speaking engagements all around Atlanta on this topic and so many more. So, consider this book "pre-marital counseling" for your business.

I guess, there is no better person to write this foreword than B. Zachary Bennett's marketing partner and partner in life – me. My hope is that this book helps you develop customers who are just as passionate about your business as you are – maybe even more so.

"LOVE IS PASSION, OBSESSION, SOMEONE YOU CAN'T LIVE WITHOUT. IF YOU DON'T START WITH THAT, WHAT ARE YOU GOING TO END UP WITH? FALL HEAD OVER HEELS. I SAY FIND SOMEONE YOU CAN LOVE LIKE CRAZY AND WHO'LL LOVE YOU THE SAME WAY BACK." — MEET JOE BLACK

Jennifer Bennett, Art Director
Reformation Productions

CHAPTER ONE

Married to Marketing

So... where to start? I often teach workshops and seminars on subjects related to Marketing and Business. And some of the people that have been attending these events have been asking me to write a book on what I've been teaching... so I think the first thing I'm going to need to do this is a great title... Married to Marketing.

Okay, so I borrowed that one from my wife. She works with me at the agency as an Art Director and when we were planning out our agency podcast, *Straight Shot*, she wanted to name it "Married to Marketing" because we were a married couple both engaged in the industry, and we talk about marketing all the time... like we were married to it as well as each other. So I want to give her credit for the name.

But I'm going to suggest that it's not just she and I who are married to marketing. All business owners are. Or at least they should be. Some may be flirting with it, wanting to take it out on dates, but never making the full-time commitment. But in order to grow a family, you need to go all in.

When you go into business for yourself, there should be some sort of premarital counseling. Some orientation that lets people know what they are signing up for. Maybe then, so many businesses wouldn't end like failed marriages.

Owning a business is a commitment. It's a commitment to a vision. It's a commitment in time. It's a commitment in money. It's a commitment to hard work. It's A LOT like marriage. And marketing is a huge part of that business... and that commitment. Marketing is business communications... and without communication, a marriage dies.

You want a fruitful marriage that people can aspire to; you want to leave a legacy that stands the test of time.. in short, you want to be successful. And that starts with understanding what you are in for.

Now, there are also other correlations like providing security through having resources - in marriage, that's being able to afford a life together, having a sharable vision, and the drive to see your commitment through no matter what. But this book is going to discuss that most important aspect of marriage - communication, aka marketing.

By the time you pick up this book to read it or show interest in its subject matter, you likely understand the fundamentals of dating and relationship building as it is observed in our society. I know that times change, so I'll confess to using the traditional views of courtship and marriage that I grew up with. This book is centered around making a correlation between that and the business world – enjoy.

CHAPTER TWO

Understanding marketing in business

There are several reasons that people own businesses: they grew up wanting to pursue a dream of doing something in a new way, or they wanted to continue growing what their father started before them, or maybe they saw great potential in something and believed they could expand the idea and take it further than others... those are the romantic notions. But there are also several businesses that were born out of necessity - - simply to pay the bills. Some are "arranged" takeovers or mergers because it simply made sense. In life, we've seen both romantic and calculated marriages to business. With any of these cases, there is one constant -if you don't have communication, the marriage (the business) will die.

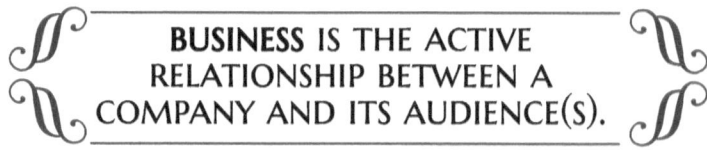

BUSINESS IS THE ACTIVE RELATIONSHIP BETWEEN A COMPANY AND ITS AUDIENCE(S).

Let's take a moment to clarify a couple of words. The word "business" refers to the active relationship between a company and its audiences. We have a tendency to interchange the words "Company" and "Business," but technically, this is incorrect. The "company" is the legal entity that conducts business, the activity. When we say "business," we are referring to the activities of the company.

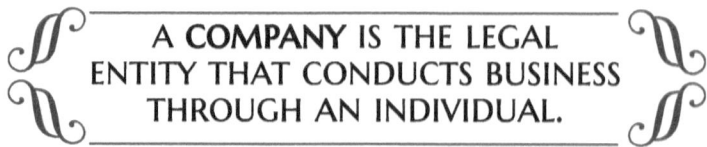

A **COMPANY** IS THE LEGAL ENTITY THAT CONDUCTS BUSINESS THROUGH AN INDIVIDUAL.

So, let's take an entrepreneurial view for a moment -you have an idea for a business - you first have to go through setting up the legal and practical aspects of setting up your company. Just like in societies' histories, when a man would prepare a home for his bride.

He would make sure he had skill and stability in his abilities to provide so that he could prove himself to be capable to his bride's family, and he would build a home for them to live in. Then, once married, he would carry her across the threshold into the new home that he had prepared. (Don't laugh. It may be old school, but it is/ was a very beautiful tradition. Remember, I did say we'd be going with a more traditional view of marriage and courtship in this analogy.)

In business, that looks a lot like preparing your foundation... before you bring your bride (the customer) into your home. Foundationally, there are certain things that must be set up. The legality of your company (LLC, Corp, etc.), securing start-up capital, getting your resources, etc., those elements will set you up to be a **legitimate** company but not necessarily a **good** business. To be a good business, you have to be set up to grow and expand before realizing success. And that is done on the back of communication.

Business communication comes through a process known as branding. You have to set up your company brand so that it can be used in communicating who you really are throughout your marriage.

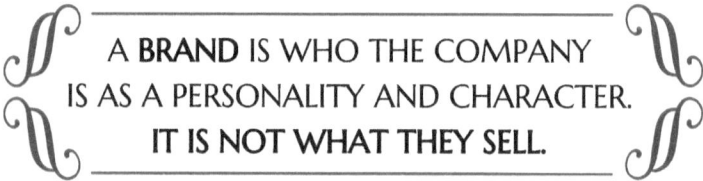

A **BRAND** IS WHO THE COMPANY IS AS A PERSONALITY AND CHARACTER. **IT IS NOT WHAT THEY SELL.**

Once you've established your brand foundation and begin your business communication (marketing), you start to see growth. That is to say that by continually wooing your bride, you may start to bear children... that's growth. Your children are the profits of your labor. And communication, just like other aspects of marital life, can definitely be considered labor at times.

BRANDING;
{ bran·ding }.

NOUN

THE PROCESS OF PROACTIVELY DEVELOPING, MANAGING, AND EXPLOITING THE PERCEPTION OF A BUSINESS IN THE MINDS OF THEIR AUDIENCE SO THAT THEY WILL REMEMBER AND CHOOSE THEM IN THE MARKETPLACE.

Continually reinvesting in your communications will make for the growth that you will need to expand your operations, which will continually drive you towards success.

A majority of your efforts will be spent communicating your business. Marketing is not an afterthought... it's the fuel that lights the fire of your business and keeps the motors turning. In this analogy, fire would be sales and motors would be operations, but perhaps that's another book - for now, we'll make it the next chapter.

The point is that marketing is going to take effort... several small business owners don't understand how much of a priority it is. As businesses fail, the divorce rate goes up.

So, why is Marketing so important? Well, let's first describe what it is. Often, the issue is that people don't really know what certain terms actually mean. Again, words matter. Marketing is just a wittier way of saying *Business Communications*. Marketing is the act of proactively communicating for the purpose of awareness, fame, sales, raising funds, or bringing celebrity. And, as I mentioned, that communication is very important.

MARKETING;
{ mahr·ki·ting }.
NOUN

THE ACT OF PROACTIVELY COMMUNICATING FOR THE PURPOSE OF AWARENESS, FAME, SALES, RAISING FUNDS, OR BRINGING CELEBRITY.

The next thing to understand is what actually communicates. In terms of business, that is practically everything. We have obvious communications, and then we also have subliminal communications. All must be taken into account.

For example, an advertisement is obvious business communication. You were obviously trying to communicate something to the reader, listener, or viewer about your company. It is obvious. But there are also subliminal communications, such as the uniform that your staff wears, that communicates to the customer in ways that are less obvious, less tangible, and more cerebral and psychological in nature. This includes things like Customer Service at a restaurant and the physical layout of a park. What are these things saying to your customers? Communication takes into effect several factors including the colors and sounds that you use, the word choice that you use, and how each of those elements impacts someone emotionally. All of these obvious and psychological factors go into trying to influence your audience through your communications. Regis McKenna, a guru in the marketing industry, is known for saying it this way: "Marketing is everything and everything is marketing." What he means by that is that everything that touches your customer is communicating to them. Every thing. And all of that communication is underneath the umbrella of marketing--business communications.

So you see marketing isn't simply about advertising, signage, and collateral materials. It is all-consuming. Marketing is concerned with the "why" behind business. It is creative, strategic, and psychological in nature. It's focus has to be centered around why consumers choose one product or service over another. And how we can influence that decision, that choice, through communicating our brand. Effective business communications take advantage of every opportunity to communicate your brand in the best ways possible towards that end.

YOUR BUSINESS

Using the relationship analogy, it's about a boy walking up to a girl, and before he ever opens his mouth, we consider: what is he communicating to her? What is the way he is dressed saying? What is the way that he smells saying? What is being communicated by the way he is standing or walking or sitting? What is the car that he drove up in communicating to the girl that he is about to approach? What is he presenting? Is it attractive to her specifically? Does he have her desired attention?

Once he approaches her and has her attention, what is he going to say in the limited amount of time that he has to influence her image of him, her understanding of him, and then finally, her decisions as they relate to him? It's courtship and making an impact using all available opportunities and resources to ensure it goes your way, in your favor.

It's the reason why people decide what they are going to wear when they go out on the town. How is the girl going to do her hair or make-up? Why the boy cleans his car before driving over to pick her up for the date. They understand that presentation is important and it's why they spend time making that a priority. It's really the first stages of relationship building - before you ever get in front of the other person.

It's simply continuous from there. After you begin a relationship, you cannot stop caring about how you present yourself. It must continue. Continuing over the lifetime of the relationship, in order to get the most out of it and reach success. We have heard about people that "let themselves go" after "getting the girl" - - these are notably recognized as failures in the relationship and looked down upon in our society. Because once you stop caring about how you are presenting yourself, you are perceived as having given up on the relationship and valuing it less than you did originally. And that communicates A LOT to the other person.

And in that, I would say that a marketing agency is like a relationship consultant. That's really what we do: provide direction and recommendations as to how a business is communicated, both in the beginning and continually in their relationship to their audiences, both potential and existing.

CHAPTER THREE

HOW MARKETING INTERACTS WITH SALES

Now, I know that you've heard of "Sales & Marketing" as if it was a single pairing. The two are, in fact, related, but they are not the same thing. At some point the word "Sales" became unpopular... mainly because people don't like to be *sold* to. When that happened, people starting tacking on "Marketing" to soften the term. While they are related, they are also completely different. Let me explain.

Marketing is communication – it's the thinking, the strategies, the visuals, the sounds, and the words behind the actions. Sales is the action – it's the feet on the street, implementing what marketing has put together. Marketing should make Sales' job easier, but it does not replace it. Sales has its own skills set the same as Marketing does.

FUEL AND FIRE

So to return to what I mentioned in the first chapter, Marketing is the spark that lights the fire that creates action through sales. You've heard people talk about the spark in a relationship and being "on fire" for something or someone. That spark ignites a passion that motivates action. That action moves the relationship forward. That explains Marketing's relationship to Sales.

Let's paint another picture - the car and the internal combustion engine: a spark plug provides the spark that ignites the fuel and causes a miniature gas explosion that moves air and forces the piston to move up or down, which turns the gears and moves the wheels that drive the car. The business owner/manager/c-level executive turns the key that starts the ignition. The spark plug is the agency that provides the spark - the ideas, strategy, and creative. The fuel is your marketing budget that is used by the spark to cause fire. The sales teams are the pistons that drive the gears that propel the company (the vehicle) forward.

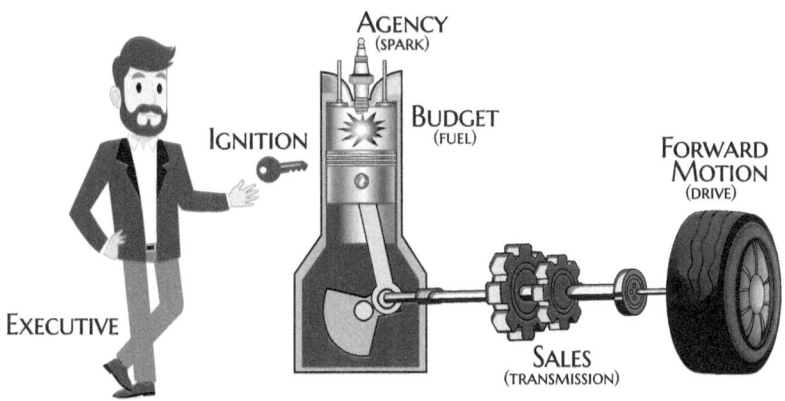

Half of my audience completely understands the picture I just painted, and the other half are lost. Let me give another analogy. This one set in Hollywood…

✳ ✳ ✳

RELATIONSHIP CONSULTANT

In the 2005 Columbia Pictures' Hollywood movie release *Hitch*, Will Smith plays the role of a dating coach who signs on a client named Albert, played by Kevin James, who hopes to win the heart of Allegra, played by Amber Valletta.

In the movie, Albert comes to Alex "Hitch" Hitchens to learn the best ways to accomplish his goals.

Hitch has built his practice by learning the art of communication with women and turning his experiences and research into tactical methods that can be shared with his clients. Now, all women are not the same, so he gathers information from Albert to access the situation and begins to make recommendations based on his expertise, observations, and insight.

The movie opens with Hitch telling the viewer his philosophies based on his experiences and research. This is his "pitch" and why someone should choose to work with him. He has a process and guidelines that he operates from:

-You cannot use what you do not have- Be you.

-Be confident. They've already said yes to meeting you - it's your job to continue that yes.

-"You" is a fluid concept- be who you need to be.

-Hang back - Don't push.

-Ask her questions to gain her perspective and insight.

-Listen and respond.

-My job is to get you to that first kiss.

By the time he meets with Hitch, Albert is already interested in Allegra. In their first meeting, Hitch begins to evaluate the circumstances as Albert shares information about Allegra and himself. From that information, Hitch begins to formulate his plan, do some research, and implement his strategy with Albert.

Steps:
1. Get her attention
2. Make the right moves
3. Be patient
4. Take it seriously
5. Course correct as necessary

Think of Marketing as the relationship consultant in the movie. In our analogy, Hitch is Marketing, Albert is Sales, and Allegra is the customer.

Now, the movie is a comedy with twists & turns that don't embrace the full picture of what I am drawing on here, but it should be enough to help the analogy. Hitch gives Albert the tools necessary to win Allegra. He crafts the story, what he needs to communicate and why, and the methods to implement the strategy in his communications. Albert then has to do the leg work. Albert is the one that's actually in the room with Allegra and has to navigate the conversations.

The main point of the movie is that it is not about manipulation. Hitch's main instruction is to be the best version of yourself, but be yourself. In the movie, Hitch says "my job is not to deceive but to create opportunities." Marketing creates opportunities for Sales to do their thing. Sales is often associated with a negative stereotype, so let me take this moment to clarify that your job as the company is not to push your product or service onto people (no one likes a pushy salesman). Your job is to find out who will benefit from your product or service and then figure out how to present those aspects to them in a way that will motivate them to remember, choose, and then prefer you in the marketplace. This is the goal of marketing.

Hitch provides the stats necessary to back up the direction he is providing and the experience to direct Albert. He stays with Albert throughout the process and helps him navigate the waters, but Albert has to do the sales himself. And those skills are a necessity. A qualified salesperson will know how to read a conversation and when to pull from what Marketing has provided him in the big picture.

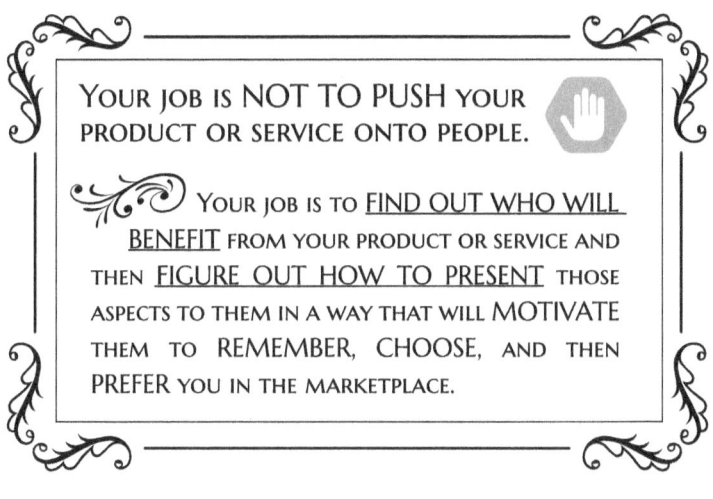

YOUR JOB IS NOT TO PUSH YOUR PRODUCT OR SERVICE ONTO PEOPLE.

YOUR JOB IS TO FIND OUT WHO WILL BENEFIT FROM YOUR PRODUCT OR SERVICE AND THEN FIGURE OUT HOW TO PRESENT THOSE ASPECTS TO THEM IN A WAY THAT WILL MOTIVATE THEM TO REMEMBER, CHOOSE, AND THEN PREFER YOU IN THE MARKETPLACE.

✳ ✳ ✳

TWO-SIDED RELATIONSHIP

However, the information flows both ways. Sales should also inform Marketing as to their experiences in the field; sharing with them what they see while on the front lines. It is not a competition as many people believe. Though both teams have the same goal, they should work together and understand each other's roles in getting to that shared goal. Both have to be humble enough to help each other.

Sales will be able to share their experience and perspectives including:

- The competitive landscape

- Common points of resistance

- Common points of interest

- Insights regarding decisions makers and purchasers

In larger organizations, the sales manager or director will be able to gain this information from his sales team and relay it to the head of marketing or Agency rep. In the same way, the CMO or agency rep will relay the information to his team for analysis and recommendations that he will then present to the company's executive team. On a smaller scale, we may simply be talking about the business's lone salesperson providing the feedback to the marketing guy or agency account representative. In either case, this insight is vital to ensuring the best strategies for the company as a whole.

It is important to recognize that these two disciplines, while both vital to company growth, are different from each other with independent experiences, skill sets, and expertise.

✳ ✳ ✳

ATTITUDE IS EVERYTHING

Let's rejoin our movie analogy and go back into some of what Hitch was revealing at the beginning of the film. What does his opening "pitch" say about Hitch/Marketing ... and how can that be reinterpreted for Albert/Sales in the world of business, so that you can "get the girl?"

~BE YOU ~
YOU CANNOT USE WHAT YOU DO NOT HAVE

The majority of people in our society can spot a fake a mile away....and they don't like it. So the best advice is to be yourself... And by "you," I mean the company brand. It is the company's responsibility to hire salespeople who can best represent the company brand so that they don't feel the need to put on a false air about themselves. And then, it is the sales person's responsibility to be honest about the company moving forward.

Salespeople must NOT promise things that the company cannot deliver. They must NOT present themselves in ways that could be considered false. For example, do not say that you have the quickest service in the industry if you do not. Don't make promises that the company's reality cannot back up.

What your marketing expert will do is help you to identify what your salespeople CAN say, so that they are always truthful and always representing the company in a good light while motivating prospective customers.

~BE CONFIDENT~
THEY'VE ALREADY SAID YES TO MEETING YOU.
IT'S YOUR JOB TO CONTINUE THAT YES

Sales should be trained to recognize and appreciate "yes." Successful sales is just a series of "yeses." The first "yes" comes when you are allowed the opportunity to present yourself at all! And your job, as a salesperson, will be to get the prospective customer/client to continually tell you yes throughout the conversation.

The good news is that, as you progress through those "yeses," your confidence can build if you recognize your moments of triumph as such. If you seem unsure, your prospect will begin to doubt, and you don't want that.

A good salesperson has the skill necessary to navigate the conversation and have the prospect continually agree with them without making it obvious that they are doing so. It's not a trick – it's a skill. Never try to trick your prospects. But you also don't want to lead them through a conversation that seems like a script where they are literally being led to say the word "yes" either. Successful salespeople understand building a conversation naturally and building a relationship that will be beneficial for both the customer/client and the company.

~BE WHO YOU NEED TO BE~
"YOU" IS A FLUID CONCEPT

Too many people stand behind "that's just the way that I am." But instead of a declaration of truth, it's an excuse for lack of planning or lack of skill.

Your branding professional will be able to lead you through defining who "you" should be. While it's important to recognize and offer up the ingredients that go into the make-up of your business, it's also just as important to not be stuck to something that isn't going to be beneficial to the company. As a company, "You" should be comprised of where you come from, what you do, how you do it, and what the customer/clients expect and desire from your business. He/She will help you develop who you should be while still ensuring that "you" are authentic and not false.

It's not really a question of genuine authenticity. People have multiple sides to who they are. My father was an Airline Pilot, a husband, a Dad, a friend, a provider, a teacher, a Christian, a conservative, a grandfather, and much more….all at the same time. He was multifaceted. Your business is the same way. We just need to make sure that the side you put facing forward is the most beneficial for both the company and the customer.

One of the reasons why this is important is that it is damaging to the bottom line if you communicate the "you" that no one cares about. Business communication isn't inexpensive, so if you spend money presenting yourself in a way that your audience doesn't relate to, you are wasting money. And in the marketing world, that's a travesty.

So have your branding/marketing professionals help determine who the company should be, and then your sales professionals will need to represent that "you" for the company in the marketplace.

~HANG BACK~
DON'T PUSH

I said it earlier and I'll likely say it again: People don't like pushy. Don't push. Pushing seems desperate, nefarious, uncouth, and amateur. Pushing is what turned people off on "sales" in general.

Instead, I agree with Hitch here: just "hang back." You should observe and then interact with purpose, confidence, and intent. There is a line between being confident and arrogant, competent to follow through and overeager, or being desperate vs being there for a purpose.

Skilled salespeople understand the nuance and how to handle it. Your job isn't to push your product onto people. Your job is to figure out what your audience needs that your business can provide, and then communicate that to them in a way that they connect with and will make you chosen and preferred in the marketplace.

~ASK HER QUESTIONS ~
GAIN HER PERSPECTIVE AND INSIGHT

So we aren't going to walk up to her with a "line." What are we going to do? Once they have agreed to give you audience, it's a great time to ask them questions and gain their perspective and insight.

This information should support and confirm what

your consumer research has shown. It should also be able to inform the company of changes within the marketplace. This is a very important aspect of the sales professional. This is why there should be an open channel between Sales and Marketing.

As the suitor (salesperson) is managing the conversation, the girl (prospective client) is telling you what they are looking for, what they are interested in, what they like and dislike, and more. Knowing the questions to ask is an important part of sales.

This is a time for inquiry. What are the questions that will provide the information that you need to build a solid opinion or strategy – get the information that you need to determine if they are a good fit and if they are, what information do you need to obtain so that you can serve them best? Again, that is your goal – to find compatibility and determine how your product/service can best serve the customer. What can you do to make their life better, more enriched? So that they, in turn, can help better your life as well. Serve to be served. Marriage/business is a two way street.

~LISTEN AND RESPOND~
It's a two-way conversation

So you are in the conversation, and it's going well. Don't forget to listen to their answers and comments. An effective salesperson will be able to take in all the information that the prospect is offering, see where it lines up with information about the company and its products/services, and then determine what they should say in response that will lead to continuing that "yes" we talked about earlier.

Again, this is skill. You can tell that I have a high respect for good salespeople. A good salesperson has to be mentally "on-their-feet" and ready to respond intelligently at a moment's notice. They have to be well informed on the state of the market, the positioning of the company, the benefits of the product/service, and the competitive landscape. And that information comes from Marketing.

~MY JOB IS TO GET YOU THAT FIRST KISS~
AFTER THAT, YOU ARE ON YOUR OWN

It is important to recognize the different roles played by Sales and Marketing. In this analogy, Hitch (Marketing) says he is there to get you (Sales) that first kiss (armed with enough information and insight to get actionable interest.) After that, you (sales) are on your own (are responsible for negotiating the deal-making terms, and following through with the promise.)

The responsibility of both sales and marketing continues after the initial opening of the door, but there is a bit of a shift here. Marketing does a lot of homework and behind the scenes to get Sales to the front door with the Customer. Then it's Sales' job, with the help of Marketing transitioning to more of a side-coach, to continue the relationship.

Thus ends our analogy with *Hitch* the movie. I could go into how his steps, as I have outlined them in this chapter, coincide with the Straight Line Marketing Process, but I haven't defined what that is for you yet. So let's move forward and do that...

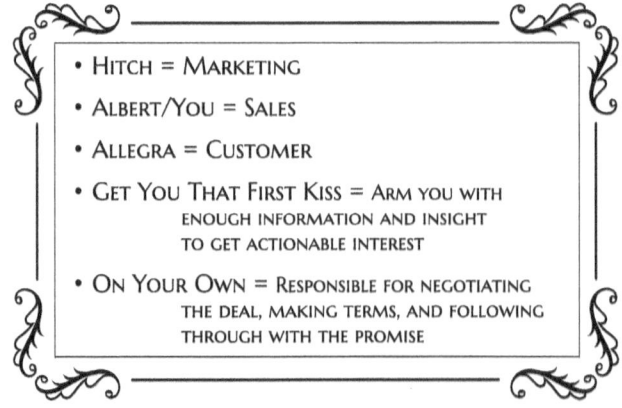

- HITCH = MARKETING
- ALBERT/YOU = SALES
- ALLEGRA = CUSTOMER
- GET YOU THAT FIRST KISS = ARM YOU WITH ENOUGH INFORMATION AND INSIGHT TO GET ACTIONABLE INTEREST
- ON YOUR OWN = RESPONSIBLE FOR NEGOTIATING THE DEAL, MAKING TERMS, AND FOLLOWING THROUGH WITH THE PROMISE

CHAPTER FOUR

THE STRAIGHT LINE MARKETING PROCESS

While working with corporate agencies, I've learned that there is a process that all agencies use with Fortune 500 companies. Each adds their own nuances and names the process differently, but common aspects stand out. Reformation Productions calls it the Straight Line Marketing Process^{tm}. It's the process of lining up who you are as a business with the desires and lifestyles of your consumers and going straight there in a more strategic manner - lining up to specific points and making the most efficient journey in a straight line. As your parents would have told you - the shortest distance between two points is a straight line. It's what connects Companies to Consumers.

There are five basic stages to the process.

1. IDENTIFY
2. LISTEN
3. THINK
4. SPEAK
5. MEASURE

We will go through each step in the relationship comparison in the coming chapters, but there are some definite principles that go before it.

* * *

DO THE HOMEWORK FIRST

I don't know if it's because people are excited, eager, lazy, or cheap, but it is in the nature of some people to try to skip steps and move ahead in line. But there are definite dangers in doing things this way. The biggest one, as it relates to business, is wasting time and money. I am very protective of these two assets for myself, for the agency, and for my clients. I despise inefficiencies because they lead to the waste of these two most valuable resources.

Why would skipping-ahead waste time and/or money? Wouldn't skipping-ahead SAVE time and/or money? Most people think this way, but it doesn't. Let me paint another picture for you:

Let's say you want to start a business in manufacturing. You are good at innovation, have the know-how to produce 'wonder products', and hire staff to help you bring your products into the marketplace. Then you spend money and effort communicating 'who you think you are' and 'what you do' to the marketplace hoping to get customers and sales.

You start strong by selling to your family & friends and your employees' families & friends, but the business isn't growing the way that it should. So you spend more money and time to communicate yourself to the marketplace and nothing is working.

You've fallen victim to "putting the cart before the horse" by skipping vital steps in the process: Brand Development and Consumer Research. Where did this waste time and money for you? Let's take a few "worst case" examples of what you risked:

- You spent time talking about what you thought was important to your customers rather than KNOWING what was important... and you were wrong. So all the money and time you spent communicating was wasted because they didn't care that you were "made in the USA," only you did.

- You built your location in a place where people aren't willing to travel. So by skipping consumer research, you didn't find out what they were/were not willing to do before you built your restaurant/store/shop and now it's going to cost you money and time to find a new location or incentivize customers to overcome the location-obstacle.

- You've been saying one thing in the marketplace and made your first impressions on your audience., but you were wrong. What you were communicating was offensive, off-putting, of no significance, or simply not motivating, and now you have to work extra hard to win back their attention... this time with the right message. Re-branding is possible but not an easy road. Many find themselves in a position where they have to rebuild themselves or overcome a bad/negative reputation.

- You were trying to save some dollars, so you started advertising in ways that you thought would be "easy"; now you've used up all your start-up marketing funds. And now, you realized your strategy and your message were wrong... too late.

- You made all of the communication tools that you believed you would need ... your website, brochures, social media, advertising, etc. ... and now, they all have the wrong messaging, and you have to correct or redesign them all so that they will work for you with the corrected branding and messaging. And of course, that is going to take both time and money - more money to correct than it would have taken to do it "correctly" the first time.

- You decided to go into business as ProductOne. It was a catchy name that you and your spouse thought of. And so, you built everything around that. Now you find that it's not the best name for you or that someone in Oregon already owns the name and now, all that time and money that went into promoting the name has been wasted because you must start again with a new name.

Do the homework first. Save yourself from making costly mistakes in the marketplace. You only get one chance at a first impression, so don't waste it. Don't spin your wheels going in a direction that has no traction. Don't spend money on things that you aren't sure will work for your product/service in your market.

PROACTIVITY

You should lead your business, not have your business pull you along behind it. Being reactionary can lead to chaos and waste. I don't subscribe to the idea of "throw it against the wall and see if it sticks." I believe in making proactive, educated decisions based on research data and rational thought.

Align yourself with the right people, make a plan, and take your business through the plan with confidence.

* * *

KNOWLEDGE IS POWER

The third, that I'll expand upon, as a philosophy behind the Straight Line Marketing Process, is that knowledge is power. I believe that wisdom and education lead people to success. Ignorance may be bliss, but it is not smart.

I spend a great deal of effort helping to educate business owners and professionals for this very reason: An informed business leader is a better business leader.

I believe in studying the successes and failures of others to gain wisdom in business. I have set Reformation Productions apart from others as being a provider of fresh ideas, creative design, and effective strategies that are designed to work against a backdrop of proven success in the traditions of business. That insight comes from studying and learning the methods, strategies, and stories of others who came before me. In my video podcast, *Straight Shot marketing podcast,* I often explore the lessons learned from other businesses and how those lessons still apply in business today.

✳ ✳ ✳

In the next few chapters, I'll guide you through each of the stages in the Straight Line Marketing Process, while using our marriage metaphor.

CHAPTER FIVE

IDENTIFYING YOUR BRAND

So let's jump into the marital comparison of business communications with the Straight Line Marketing Process by talking about preparing for that first date with your potential bride - the customer.

Before you become engaged, there are several things you have to figure out: Who are you? What do you want? What are you looking for? This is a time of preparing yourself for the possibility of marriage. If you were to have a pre-marital counselor break down the psychological process, we would find several similarities between business and marriage.

SELF DISCOVERY

In this first stage of the process, we explore where you come from – what's your legacy. Is there anything in your history that makes you more suitable for success than others? What are your goals apart from that history? What do you seek to accomplish in the marketplace? What makes you different from all the other suitors that are looking to court your future bride? This is a time of total self-discovery. Not total for you as an individual but for you as a business. Like I mentioned earlier in regards to *Hitch*, "you" is a very fluid concept. This is where we first start to determine who "you" will be from a business standpoint. So just like the bride's father is going to look at you, you need to step outside of your individual self and look at yourself as a possible son-in-law, as a provider for his daughter, the continuation of a family legacy, and the provider of his grandchildren. We examine and prepare the business from every possible vantage point.

During this phase of marital preparation, the suitor starts on his own. This is a time of self-reflection and goal setting. So you are encouraged to think as much as you can about yourself during this time. This IS the selfish phase. This is when girls dream about the husband they will one day land, and boys dream about how they will swoop in on horseback to save the girl from certain doom (life with the other available suitors). Dream. Dream as much as you can. This is the time. This is where those dreams start to become more formed goals in the face of reality. Explore ideas. Think through possibilities. Begin to shape who you are going to become.

Why is this important? Well, before you can love someone else, you have to be able to love yourself. You need surety and confidence that can only come from self-discovery. You want people to look at you and say "You see him/her? They have it together. They know who they are and what they want." This knowledge of self will help guide your path.

You need to determine what matters to you. What are the pieces of character that you are going to stake your life on? What are "deal breakers" that you cannot accept from yourself or from others? What are the areas where you would be willing to compromise? There is an old cliché my wife loves to use with our children: "Stand for something, or you'll fall for anything." This is the time where you determine what you are going to stand for. Your bride is looking for a man with character and the strength of knowing who they are.

COMPETITIVE ANALYSIS

But knowing yourself isn't enough; you also need to know your competition. During this self-discovery, you are developing who you are, but you have to have a fuller picture before stepping out into the world. Let's look at the others in town that are looking to become married. The young man down the street is the president of the class, he's the son of the mayor, and the captain of the football team – how are you going to compete with him? You must have an answer. In the movie *The Godfather*, Don Corleone advises to "keep your friends close and your enemies closer." This statement is about knowledge. You can't be scared of your competition. Observe them, study them, learn them, and strategize how you are going to make a difference in the marketplace. What would make the most sought after girl in town choose to make a life with you? What makes you different, and is that difference going to matter in her eyes?

You should take stock of who the other players are, and then be honest about what they are offering in comparison with yourself. Where do you stand? What can you do to improve your situation as a suitor?

KEEP YOUR FRIENDS CLOSE

AND YOUR ENEMIES CLOSER

* * *

CUSTOMER INSIGHTS

Not only should you think about your competition, but you should consider your potential customers as well. Who do you want to marry? What type of person are you looking for? Just as you looked into your own character to determine what you would or would not stand for, what are the elements that are a must in their character? What are areas that you might be willing to compromise on? Let's brainstorm for a minute, what are some character traits that you feel are necessary in your spouse?

- Do they have to be kind?

- Do they need to be charitable?

- Do they need to have drive (be more aggressive) or do you want them to be more laid back and relaxed?

- Do you want someone who is independent or someone you can take care of that feels they *need* you?

- There are no wrong answers. All of these character

traits should complement your own character traits. Should they be like you, or do you believe that opposites attract?

Beyond character traits, what are some of the more physical or worldly traits that matter to you?

- Should they be able to support a family?

- Should they be able to contribute financially to the family?

- Do you want a spouse who stays at home and focuses on raising children?

- Do you want someone who is tall or short?

- How do you feel about their body type?

- Would it be okay with you if they shared their opinion on how you are put together?

You need to be able to look at all the possibilities, even the ones that aren't polite to discuss, because you need to face the truth. Owning and operating a business is difficult, just like marriage, and the sooner you recognize the truth of a situation, the better off you will be. You need to walk into the marketplace with your eyes open.

After you start to build a picture of who the perfect spouse would be, what do you think they do? Where do they live? How will you find them? Spend some time thinking about this from your own viewpoint. Where do you think they are? What do you think they do? We'll ask them soon enough, but what are your initial thoughts?

✳ ✳ ✳

ASPIRATIONS

What are your aspirations and desires? What are your goals in life? What are your goals for the marriage? Like I said, now is the time to dream. Put those thoughts into the universe and on paper. What do you want for your future?

If one of your goals is to truly make a difference in your industry, then you will need to operate your business in such a way that concentrates on moving the needle for your peers. But if you are simply wanting to work for yourself and not have a "boss" until you retire, that will be a different outlook on your business. Or maybe you want to build a legacy business that you can pass on and provide for your children and their children, etc.

It's important to recognize your visions and set goals so that you don't end up 20 years into your marriage and say to yourself "Why am I here?" or "What have I done?" in some negative way. Marrying the wrong person can set your life off course and cause heartache, financial drain, and delays in experience. The same risks are in business.

THE TRUTH

If you were your customer, would you choose to marry one of the other suitors or yourself? Are the differences that you bring to the table those that matter most?

It is important to be honest with yourself. Now's the time to explore it all – the good, the bad, and the ugly. There are several questions that you need to ask yourself and really face the music on:

1. DO YOU WANT IT BAD ENOUGH TO ADJUST WHAT YOU ENVISION PERSONALLY?

   It doesn't matter what YOU want to do and how

YOU want to be known if the marketplace isn't interested in it….. because YOU won't be able to stay in business without THEM.

If you want to be known as the one who "wears the pants" in the family, the strong arm and decisive element, the "what I say goes" type of person, but your spouse doesn't have the same vision for your role – you will not be married for long. It is important to recognize what areas you are willing to adjust in order to be successful in your business/marriage.

2. Is it worth it?
   At the same time, it's important to be honest with yourself about what you want your business to be so that you are not wasting your time chasing someone else's dream instead of your own, even if the marketplace is asking for it.

   If you've always wanted a big family and your spouse doesn't, you need to determine if this is an area you are willing to compromise on? If not, you might have a miserable marriage.

3. Can you stand up to the competition?
   It is important to recognize if you possess the

marketplace differences that are going to matter. If you are going to be overpriced in the marketplace, you need to know that so you can address it.

Consider all the young studs out there looking to get married and think about what is going to make you stand out as a preferred choice for that special someone. Remember, they have to choose you as much as you have to choose them. And remember, people have a right to choose... even if their choice is not to choose.

4. DO YOU HAVE THE DRIVE?
   I am very honest with entrepreneurs when I meet them and remind them that owning a business is hard work. It takes a lot of character and stamina to be successful in the marketplace. I tell them, I can guide you in what you should do, but I can't make you do it. In the end, that has to come from you.

   It's similar to how parents try to raise their children to choose the "right kind of mate." We can guide, instruct, and intervene as much as we possibly can but in the end, it's their life... and their choice.

   I believe that in America, you can do anything you

set your mind on if you have the drive and put in the work. There are simply too many rags-to-riches stories that support this in our country. But drive is a very important element in each of them.

5. Do you have the resources?
You can't prepare a mansion for you and your spouse to move into once you're married if you don't have the resources. You have to find a way to either gain the resources or compromise on where you want to begin until you can make that house happen for your family.

In business, capital often comes from savings that you've accumulated over your previous work history, raising funds with investors, getting a loan through a bank, obtaining a grant from the government or other organization, the SBA, prize money, etc. There are many paths available, but you have to be able to build your house before you can live in it.... and that is going to take money. Be honest about what you have available to you, so you can plan with that in mind.

Be realistic about your budget. Don't make assumptions or set policies based on "hopes" of what might happen. Often business plans get criticized by loan officials and investors for being built on "and by then we should be making a million dollars so ..." Make sure you are building your plan based on realistic goals and expectations; true resources and abilities; and sound strategic thinking.

These are all areas where you need to be truly honest with yourself and recognize the details in these areas so that you can plan for them proactively – build a strategy with these elements in mind, and you are on the road to success.

CHAPTER SIX

LISTENING TO YOUR CUSTOMERS

The previous chapter was all about you – your perceptions, thoughts, visions, expectations, characteristics, etc. This chapter is all about your spouse. Here, they are the focus. While knowing yourself is important, vital even, relationships are not one-sided.

Let's take a walk through the more recognized steps in relationship building. Walk with me in your mind as we go through these phases, one at a time, with our comparative analogy.

* * *

DATING

So, you now know yourself, and you are ready to start dating. It's time to see how those internal thoughts match up in the real world. It's time to "put yourself out there" and see if you can find a Yin to your Yang.

I've always thought of dating as basically a series of interviews, with different people you find interesting, for the role of spouse. In this mindset, if you find that the person you are on a date with is incompatible, you should stop seeing them … because you are wasting resources. Not only yours, but theirs as well. Time, money, energy, passion, and emotion are all precious resources and should be treated as such for both parties.

Now, I've been just as guilty as anyone else in wasting these resources as a young person.

- Staying with the wrong person out of fear of being alone.

- Spending money with the wrong person because you wanted to fit in.

- Acting passionate for someone because other people liked them and thought you should be with them.

It's part of growing up. But you only live once, and none of us have the promise of tomorrow. The more time and effort that you spend on someone who is not going to be your spouse, the less time and money you will have to devote to finding and then living with "the one."

YOUR BUSINESS MARRIAGE

So to keep from waste, you need to keep in mind your end goal when dating. With that in mind, you are on a quest for data that will help you determine the rest of your life. Dating, in this definition, is very basic and surface-level. We aren't talking about diving deep into who the person is - that comes later. You have to walk before you can run.

To date successfully, you have to know where to meet the type of women/men you are interested in. To do so, we need to determine several aspects:

- WHAT DO THEY LOOK LIKE?
  No matter what people tell you, all individuals are different. And differences are good. But you can begin to identify the differences in people and categorize them so that you can begin to determine some sort of profile for the type of person you are looking for.

- WHERE DO THEY HANG OUT?
  You can't expect them to come to you. You have to go to where they are and mingle.

DATING = DATAING

In the business world, we get this information from profiling existing customers in our industry. Those are the people we are interested in. If you are an existing business, you can use your existing customers as a map for building new customers just like them. If you are a new business, you can look at the customers of other businesses, who purchase similar products/services in your industry. This information gives you a starting place. You can also target potential customers with social media. Here several people will list their interests, and we can utilize that information to get to the right people.

IF OUR ANALOGY WAS WITH FISHING,
WE WOULD CALL THIS FISHING IN A STOCKED POND...
BUT IT ISN'T, SO IGNORE THAT.

In the dating stage, we are looking to move from your own thoughts into more detailed and defined data, based on research.

✳ ✳ ✳

GOING TOGETHER

Vocabulary changes throughout the years. When my father was a young man, they called it "going steady". My daughter's generation calls it "going out." But we called it "going together." You've dated many others trying to find "the one", and you've found someone that you want to get to know more deeply and become exclusive with. You won't date anyone else, and neither will they.

Now's the time to REALLY get to know them as a person – find out what makes them tick. Why they do certain things? What are their core values? What do they think of your core values? In the business world, we call these elements a customer's demographics, media habits, and lifestyle habits.

We want to test, confirm, or adjust our own

thoughts on who our customers are based on our experiences in this stage of relationship building.

So, just like in relationship building, not everyone follows the same steps in business, but there are several options and steps available depending on the situations. The principles are the same, regardless of how you accomplish the tasks.

In the first chapter, I briefly mentioned a "made in the USA" experience I had with a client at Reformation Productions. Let me expand upon that as it relates to this section of the book. I had a client who was sure that the fact that her products were made in America was a premium selling point. It really mattered to her in her own thoughts, and so she assumed that it mattered to her customers. She had spent many dollars and several years, before working with us, to promote this fact.

When we engaged her customers, we found out that being made in the USA was not a factor in their decision making. The business was engaged in what is known as Bolshevik Marketing. It's a term used to describe the idea that you are promoting something based on what you think they OUGHT to care about as opposed to what really matters to the customers. The issue with this, in a free-market, capitalist society, is that it means you are wasting money saying something to customers that will not influence them to buy your product.

In this case, we were able to determine what product factors and brand differentiators DID influence the customers' decision making process and course correct the client's strategy moving forward.

As a business, that's what this "going together" time period is all about - determining why people purchase products/services like yours and what we can do to influence them to choose you in the marketplace.

Let's look at the plot of the movie *Big* starring Tom Hanks. This movie was about a boy named Josh who makes a wish at a carnival, and when the wish is granted, he wakes up with the body of an adult. He finds himself needing money to survive as an adult (don't we all) and ends up getting a job at a toy manufacturer, MacMillan Toys.

While sitting in a meeting where they are showcasing a promising new toy, he questions WHY anyone would want to play with the prototype that was being presented. No one is able to answer his question convincingly, so he makes recommendations. After this, his job quickly becomes consumer research - where he works to determine why someone would want to purchase prototype toys, to better determine if they will be successful in the marketplace. Doing so saves the company money because they won't be producing, promoting, or then discarding toys that won't sell in the marketplace. It's like doing your homework and studying before trying to take the test – you won't waste the test registration fee.

In this stage, we are trying to determine some of the same things. Why would someone choose to buy from your business? What can we say or/and do that will influence a potential customer to choose you in the marketplace?

We are also gathering information about their lives that we can utilize in determining additional ways that we will be able to make a substantial impact on them. Marketing is the study of WHY customers make purchasing decisions and HOW we can best influence those decisions. It is a hybrid combination of psychology, strategy, and creativity in business.

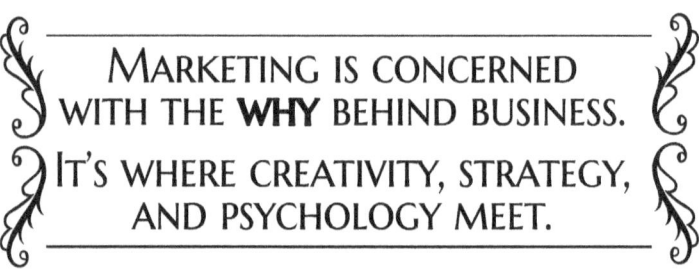

MARKETING IS CONCERNED WITH THE **WHY** BEHIND BUSINESS. IT'S WHERE CREATIVITY, STRATEGY, AND PSYCHOLOGY MEET.

When you are going steady with your significant other, you need to find out this level of detail before you entertain the idea of taking them down the aisle. If you are incompatible, stop. If you need to make adjustments in your thinking, do it. Marriage is a big commitment. Entering the marketplace as a business is, too.

In the same way that no one seeks to enter a marriage and watch it fail, no one starts a business expecting to fail. The time and energy you invest in the front-end of the relationship will make things more fruitful/ profitable throughout. Success often comes from doing the homework up front.

C H A P T E R   S E V E N

THINKING OUT YOUR MESSAGING AND STRATEGY

So you've been going together for quite some time. Now it's time for you to make some decisions. You need to endure deep contemplations because this is where the rubber meets the road. This is where you put your good money down. You decide to "take the plunge" – you are going to commit. So you continue investing in your marriage by making a large singular purchase - the ring. The ring is a tradition that says "I'm in it to win it," "I'm serious," and "I'm ready."

Are you ready? In business, this is the time when we take all of the information that we've gathered before now and figure out what they mean in light of each other. You've spent time on yourself as a business, your dreams, aspirations, character, position in the marketplace, etc. And you've spent time on your customers, determining what they want in the marketplace; what they like and dislike; where they live, work, and play; and how you can interact with them. Now is the time to start laying the foundation.

= *Commitment*
= *Dedication*
= *Loyalty*
= *Understanding*
= *Recognition of Responsibility*

✳ ✳ ✳

ENGAGEMENT

So you're engaged... that's awesome! There is so much to celebrate in this time period... but there is even more to do. Now is the time when we really get serious. It's time to determine how you'll be able to fulfill each other's dreams and meet each others' needs. Businesswise this is the same as asking "what is your strategy?" But it's also time to plan the wedding ceremony and how you are going to present yourselves to the world as a married unit.

~REPRESENTATION~

At this point, you know yourself, and you know your spouse. Now is the time to start thinking about the collective "you." Who are you to be as a married couple, as a family? What do you want your family to mean to others? We need to establish a vision, so we can develop the plan to fulfill it. The brand message comes from the previous work (described in Chapters 5 and 6), and everything after will come out of this development.

In business, we call this your **Messaging**. It's

basically the answer to: What do you want your business to say to other people? To other businesses? How do you want to be remembered? What will your legacy be? What will people say about you when you are brought up in conversations?

In both marriage and business, it's important that you be honest and truthful in determining what your messaging will be. If you build your message, your legacy, on something that you can't substantiate, it will come out... and chances are good that it will do damage.

Think about Sid and Nancy, Will and Jada Pinkett Smith, Brad and Angelina, JFK and Jackie, ... What comes to mind when you think about those couples? WHO are they? What do/did they mean to you from the outside looking in?

Now, in the same vein, think about Apple, Google, Coca-Cola, Ford, Ferrari... What comes to mind about them outside of what they sell?

~PRESENTATION~

If representation is the internal image, then the physical image is part of presentation. And the first presentation of your marriage comes at the wedding. "Now I present to you Mr. and Mrs...." And there you are for the world to take in and reflect on. Couples spend a lot of time during their engagement dedicated to structuring that first presentation. That first presentation has elements that will crossover into the marriage. Many start planning the wedding before they even find their spouse! With the modern wedding, there are many decisions to make:

- Wedding Colors
- Wedding Party Attire
- Decorations
- Seating arrangements
- Transportation
- Name

In business, we are looking to establish the brand voice, the creative look and feel that will communicate the brand moving forward, and the concept for the next campaign.

Brand Voice refers to the tone that your brand will use in communicating with both your internal audience and your external audiences. Your voice needs to fit well with your messaging. Should your tone by aggressive, friendly, confident, directing, or submissive? Should you use a higher vocabulary, educated lexicon, or slang?

The **creative look and feel** is important for both consistency and effective communications. This area includes everything from selecting fonts that communicate your messaging visually to effective use of color and imagery.

The **campaign concept** will take both of those elements with a witty, creative idea or motif that will be explored to communicate your business for as much time as possible. Campaigns change from time to time, but well-built brands are constant. Your brand is 'who you are'. The campaign is the manner in which you choose to communicate your brand.

Chick-fil-a is a company whose brand represents wholesome, family fun, integrity, quality, and Christian ethics. They choose to communicate that through a 'cows campaign.' The campaign is part of their presentation to their public, but the brand is also showcased in their business operations and policies by being closed on Sundays to show respect to their employees, using premium condiments to showcase quality, and more.

~OPERATIONS~

The internal is ready, the presentation is prepared, now it's time to think about action. How is everything going to work together towards the established goal? In a wedding, there are a lot of moving parts:

- Who is going to officiate?

- Who is going to be in the Wedding party?

- In the wedding party, what roles are going to be assigned to whom?

- What music is going to play?

- What ceremony is going to be used?

- How are you getting to the Wedding?

- How will you be leaving the Wedding?

- Is there a Honeymoon? Where? When? How much?

In business, the questions that we ask are answered with the Strategic Marketing plan. Those questions include:

- How are we going to showcase and communicate the brand?

- Where are we going to meet with the public?

- How can we interact with the public?

- Are there any other brands that we can partner with?

- What other opportunities are available to us to make a positive impact on our brand?

With these questions answered and strategies set in place, it's time for the fun, creative tasks of marketing. It's time to build the tools that will represent who you are to your audience and take them to the stage for all to see.

CHAPTER EIGHT

SPEAKING YOUR TRUTH

You've had all the deep-rooted, meaningful conversations. It's important that you don't skip these elements because they are truly the operational foundations of your marriage, but now it's time for action. It's time for the physical foundations that showcase your thoughts and plans. This is where the bride starts to get excited, and the anticipations start to gear up.

* * *

PREPARING FOR THE DATE

You've completed a lot of rather cerebral and behind-the-scene elements, but you also have to think about the day AFTER the wedding. Where are you going to go? How are you going to live? In ancient times, it was common for a man to literally build his house during the engagement period. Now in modern times, it's more than likely selecting and then purchasing a home. When choosing where your family will operate from, you also have to look at the interior of the home. Not just the shell of the home but also the furniture and décor inside of it. How are the rooms to be utilized? How will you maintain the lawn? How are you planning to entertain guests? So many questions ...

In business, your website is your real estate on the internet. So in our comparison, obviously, you are going to have to build out that real estate. Not just the location (which is the domain name) but also the home itself. How many rooms will you have? How will they function? Who will use them? You want your home to truly represent who you are and to be an efficient place for you to operate from.

You also have to be concerned with your physical, real-world housing as well - your offices or, in some cases, your storefront. Depending on the business, many start out in a home office, progress to shared space, then to leased space, before possibly building or owning their business location. Many first time marriages start out in rented apartments or houses as well.

In both digital and physical worlds, the following matters. The couple is going to want a home that represents who they are and what is important to them, what is going to make their work and operations easiest for them, so that they can be as productive as possible both individually and as a couple. One wants an island in the kitchen because she feels it will help her with preparing meals. The other wants to ensure they have a back deck with room for a grill, table, and chairs for entertaining friends. Everyone comes into the situation with their own wants and needs. The important thing is to remember both parties. And in our comparison here, remember that the customer is the bride... and their needs are very important in the new home, just as important as the groom's (our business owner's) needs. If the bride doesn't want to stay there, the groom is going to have a problem maintaining the marriage on his own.

Beyond housing, you also need to think about transportation. Maybe that motorcycle isn't going to be as conducive for a new family all year long. If you are planning on having children right away, you'll need to consider a four-door car or larger. There are many factors to consider.

And there are many tools to help you run your household that you will need to consider: your flatware, lawnmower, china, garden hose, dishes, cookware, refrigerator, clothes washing machine, clothes dryer, can opener, coffee maker, dishwasher, stove, oven, window treatments, bed linens, towels, rugs, etc. And they all need to be considered with both parties in mind. Now is the time to make sure you have everything that is going to be necessary for the day you walk into your home for the first time together.

There any many tools in business communications/ marketing as well. You have to consider if you need a certain uniform for your employees, brochures, radio spots, TV commercials, web videos, social media, sales presentations, folders, logos, etc. In this stage, we prioritize all the tools & strategies and then create everything that is going to be necessary before the business' official launch date - the wedding presentation.

You will also need to make sure that you can afford on-going expenses. In a home, this would include electricity, water, sewage, rent/mortgage, internet/cable, etc. Many of these on-going expenses are the same in a business but additionally include digital media content, social media engagement, media communications, web content updates, reprints, inventory, staffing, etc.

All of this has to be considered, thought out, and prepared BEFORE the wedding. Shotgun weddings only lead to chaos and playing catch-up for the first several years of your marriage. They also run a higher risk of failure and divorce. I have developed relationships with several *SCORE*[1] mentors and do a good amount of business education to try to encourage business owners and entrepreneurs to avoid this huge mistake. Always plan out what you are going to do, and make sure you have the resources necessary to see your business through to success. I have seen several businesses fail and lose everything that they had invested due to a lack of planning. Planning is key.

In the early years of Reformation Productions, I helped build the brand for a destination restaurant[2]. I had worked with major restaurants earlier in my career, and I love the concepts behind many destination restaurants, so I was excited! The adult prom concept was strong, the accomplished chef was very talented, and the passionate business owner had zeal, but three months into the launch of the restaurant, when the initial buzz in the marketplace was over, she told me that they had run out of money and had to close their doors.

People who came to the restaurant loved it, so what was the problem? Well, there were many factors, but the biggest issue was a lack of planning.

This business was referred to me by a business planner who had walked the owner through starting their business. Unbeknownst to me, they overlooked one MAJOR element: In preparing to launch their business, they needed to reserve enough money to operate, without profit, for the amount of time that it would take for the business to become known in the marketplace.

Many business owners feel like they need to keep

their financial matters close to the vest, I get it. But they should have been informed that the majority of restaurants fail in their very first year. Statistically speaking, according to a frequently cited study by Ohio State University, only 40% of new restaurants make it past their first anniversary.

For this reason, all businesses, but especially restaurants, need to make sure they have enough funds to operate without substantial profit for a defined amount of time before opening their doors. It takes a while for you to get your feet under you and for you to let the public know about your business so that it can become self-supporting. Hollywood won't tell you that, but I will.

Outside of the launch, this company did not have the funds to tell the public about their restaurant. They simply hoped that the short launch would be enough to snowball success, but sadly, when it didn't, they lost everything: the money they invested in the building, staff, legal set-up, branding, all of it ... because of lack of planning.

Since that experience, I have made sure to always have that difficult financial conversation with business entrepreneurs upfront to ensure they have enough capital to start their business. If they don't, we address it immediately in the planning stage. It breaks my heart to see potentially good businesses fail.

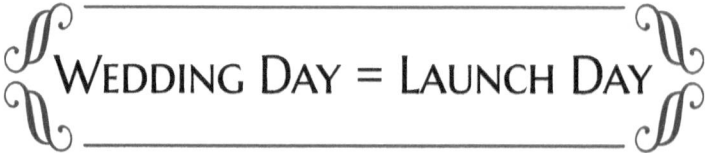

WEDDING DAY = LAUNCH DAY

* * *

THE WEDDING

You've completed all your planning. All of the necessary preparations have been made. All the tools are ready. It's finally time for the wedding. In this singular event, you will be making vows to your bride and presenting yourself to the world as a married couple.

In business, this is the launch date. The day when you complete your ribbon cutting, tell your prospective customers why they should choose you and what you are going to do for them, and present who you are to the industry. It's the great unveiling, when you open your doors to the outside world.

Several businesses don't understand the value of having a formal launch. Instead, they seek to release elements as they are available instead of building up anticipation and releasing everything simultaneously. At no time do I recommend this approach. However, I do recognize different methods for entering the marketplace.

~SOFT LAUNCH ~

A **soft launch** is a low-key, non-promoted business opening or beginning. Often, it is a pre-launch opening of sorts. There can be many reasons that we might recommend a soft launch ahead of an official launch. The biggest reason would be to gain a foundational customer base prior to the "real launch." In our analogy, this would be akin to "living together" as a couple before getting married. In this stage, a business is trying things without having made the public commitment. Maybe you are testing products and communication strategies in the market on a smaller scale before investing in a larger launch of a brand or product. This is often called "test marketing" or "pre-release." This approach allows us to collect testimonials and feedback from early customers. Those elements are then used to support or revise the official launch, or hard launch.

~HARD LAUNCH ~

The official launch, sometimes called a "**hard launch**" when preceded by a "soft launch," is when the brand/product is actually released to the general public. When all the work is done, this is throwing the first pitch of the game. It's the wedding date when you make your commitment public and present yourself to the world.

The importance of an official launch date involves creating a great first impression for your audience. It's been said a million times, but you only get one chance at a first impression. During that first impression, your prospective customers' minds are most clear of expectations and pre-judgments regarding your brand. We want everything to be perfect and in place with no holes so that we can make the most of this initial time period.

The important thing is to not try a hybrid mix of these approaches. This comes across as amateur and chaotic. Pretending to be married when you are not, and then having a wedding will only confuse your audience. That is to say that it takes away from the wonder and congratulations of your getting-married if you have already been calling your significant other your husband/wife for months or years before having a wedding. But as we know, this happens in relationships and it also happens in business.

~No Wedding ~

As history has taught us in relationships, making a public commitment isn't the only factor in success. Some couples choose to never have a ceremony. In like fashion, many businesses will indeed "take it as it comes" and not have a launch at all – that is, they never open with fanfare and celebration. But they must recognize that in doing so, they are not going to receive the wedding gifts and recognition that comes naturally from having a wedding. In business, we call that missed opportunity.

THE INVITATIONS

So you've laid your foundation. Made all the necessary decisions about whether to have a wedding or not. If you decided on having a wedding, you are now ready for the big date. So it's time for your first outreach as a couple – the invitations. Who are you going to invite? And then how are you going to invite them?

Using insights and experiences from both Bride and Groom, you will begin to build an invitation list. In business, this will be built on your targeted consumer profile and those that are most likely to support your marriage in its earliest stages.

Then, HOW are you going to invite them? This is also part of your strategy.

- Do you use traditional, mailed invitations? If so, on what type of paper stock, using what fonts, etc.? What are these invitations going to say to your prospective audience about who you are as a couple?

- Maybe you are going to telephone a few close personal friends or invite them in person?

- Maybe you will take the modern approach and send emails, evites, or video invitations?

- Perhaps you will try something even more

creative, memorable, and out-of-the-box?

These decisions are made based on how you want to present yourself and what will make the best, positive impact on your prospective guests.

When a brick-and-mortar business is opening, they will often have a grand opening and will make the announcement through direct mail or advertising. There are a multitude of ways that this can be achieved, but, in all cases, you have to know where you will find these potential, initial guests.

This revisits the idea of consumer research. A couple will start trying to obtain the addresses of their potential guests (usually by asking other guests and family). They will start asking for the opinions of their closest "sure thing" guests on how the invitations should look – often the wedding party and their families.

With business you have to know the same information:

- Who do you want to invite?
- How do we design the invitations to appeal to them and influence them to attend?

- Where are we going to be able to interact with these potential guests in order to invite them?

* * *

LAUNCH DAY

So it has come down to the day. You've done your preparation, invited your guests, and you're ready to put things into action. There are three major sections to the wedding day.

~The Ceremony~

The wedding ceremony to a business would be like the ribbon cutting to a new office, restaurant, IPO, etc. There are roles to play at this ritual.

- In our analogy, let's say that the officiant or minister is the marketing agency or the CMO. He has worked with the couple (Bride – consumer and Groom – company) to help ensure they are compatible and ready for the life to come. He has worked to help in planning the event, and he will be there to help counsel the couple moving forward when times are good and when times are rough.

- The wedding party might represent employees that are there to help the company operate on a day-to-day basis. They are members of the inner-circle that will be closest to seeing the couple's success.

- The couple's families might represent the investors and advisors that have helped shape them and whom they will be able to count on moving forward.

- And the myriad of other guests are there as people that will help support the company as they journey from this day forward.

Traditionally, guests are invited to a wedding to lay witness to the sacred vows, to show support for the marriage, and to provide accountability to them living out those vows moving forward. They take part in the covenant as well. So using those analogies, who you invite matters.

~The Reception~

The reception is a celebration of the event and the new marriage. In business, this might be the launch party, IPO party, ribbon cutting, or grand opening event.

At this point in the day, you are the host. You walk around the group, mingling, meeting, and greeting all the guests. You thank them for their support and assure them you will not let them down. They want what is best for you, and they are there to help you succeed.

As a thank you, the couple with often provide entertainment for their guest. A band or DJ may be hired. In business, there might be a celebrity appearance, company mascot, bouncy house, clowns, etc.

There are often party favors that are provided to guests. In business, we call these tchotchke or promo items.

You can see there really are quite a few similarities.

~THE CONSUMMATION~

The day ends with the sacred consummation of the marriage. In most states, the marriage isn't valid until it is consummated.

In our analogy, the first business transactions – those sales or contract agreements - would represent the intimate act of consummation. I often tell new companies, if money doesn't change hands in exchange for your offerings, then you aren't in business.

Many a marriage has been nullified on the grounds that it was never consummated. Many businesses have failed to launch from lack of initial sales.

LIVING LIFE

When the party is over, everyone has left the reception, and you've crossed the threshold with your bride, it's time to get down to the day-to-day business of being a married couple. All of your strategies and plans are put into place, and you begin writing and telling the story of your life together.

Any good marriage counselor will tell you to treat every day as special, to continue dating after you are married, and to be willing to compromise with your spouse when necessary to have a successful marriage.

In business, we would interpret that as keeping a passion for your business and maintaining consistent drive and work ethic – always striving for excellence in everything that you do. Be true to yourself/brand and your spouse/customers. Always listen to your customers/spouse and make adjustments as necessary to maintain harmony between you. Seek to grow together and expand your family when it's appropriate. Tell your story.

~The Everyday~

One of the biggest issues in marriage comes from losing focus, losing passion, and losing drive. Business is the same way. Wandering eyes can end businesses just as quickly as they can end marriages. Keep your promises. Stay true to who you are.

Now is a good time to talk about Coca-Cola. I live in Atlanta, GA – the home of Coca-Cola. They have a very strong brand, and every soft drink in the south is considered a "coke" regardless of who makes it.

However, in the mid-80s, the people at Coke changed who they were and their main product to be more like their competitor, Pepsi-Cola. Coke has always been a wholesome, fun-loving family brand centered around refreshment from hard work and life while Pepsi has always been more youthful and edgy. Coke's decision to change their formula to taste more like Pepsi was edgy, and it backfired on them with their spouse kicking them out of the house. They recoiled, went back to their roots, and their spouse let them back in the house. Both determined to make their marriage work.[3]

~KEEP COMMUNICATION~

How many times have we heard spouses complaining that "they just won't talk to me" and/or "you never listen?" A marriage therapist might say, "When is the last time you two went on a date?" That is because communication is vital to a successful relationship, and when you were dating, there was good conversation that led to your decision to be together in the first place.

If they aren't talking to you, they are talking about you. People gossiping about the opposite sex is an age-old pastime, and it doesn't stop when you get married. The question is are you involved in the conversation? Are you shaping and influencing these conversations or just being silent and allowing other people to determine who you are in the minds of others? Without the company's influence in the marketplace, people are likely to dislike them or not know them at all. "Oh, she keeps to herself; no one really knows much about her." So she is ignored. Or worse yet, people are talking about you, tearing you down, or misleading others and you stay silent, not telling your side of the story. People are going to talk, so it's important that you stay in the conversation.

To make a marriage work, you have to know your spouse. Know what they want. Know what makes them tick. Part of your "job" is to know your significant other better than anyone else so that you can provide for them in ways that no one else could. It's the same in business. You should know your customers better than any other company, any other brand. So well, that you know exactly how they need to be interacted with, serviced, treated, etc. You want your marriage to be so strong that there is no chance that another could swoop in and tempt them to leave.

When you have a strong relationship with your bride, she can provide you with insight into your own life, your own self. Allow them to help. There is not a better advocate for your brand than your best customers. They can let you know how they are feeling about the changes you have been making as a company, how you are being perceived in the marketplace, and among their friends. They can also be so overfilled with love that they sing your praises to others, building your consumer base.

When things aren't going well, sometimes a man or woman will go to their spouse's friends to ask what the other is saying about them during conversations. Businesses can do that too. Embrace the market. Ask the best friend if what you are doing is what your bride really needs or wants. Test the marketplace with new ideas, innovations, and strategies.

~COMPROMISE~

Don't bend on who you are, but make concessions. Don't be bullheaded; it's not all about you. The brand is now the boss.

Once you get married, you have to consider the sanctity of your union. Your brand should be treated the same. Back to Coca-Cola: they didn't realize just how strong their brand was or how loyal their consumer base was. So when they betrayed it, they felt the pain, and then, they compromised. They brought back "old coke" as *Coca-Cola Classic* while keeping New Coke on the market as well. They made a concession. Eventually, they determined that their spouse was right and quietly removed New Coke from the marketplace, but the two ran together for quite some time. Their bride loved the marriage and what it had come to mean in the marketplace.

Coke had done such a good job with branding that they had become part of the fabric of people's lives. New leadership in the company didn't recognize that and started to make irrational decisions that could have brought the marriage to its knees. Lesser companies have died for much less.

CHAPTER NINE

MEASURING YOUR SUCCESS

One of the most telling activities in business is measuring your success. Only through actively tracking your progress and failures are you able to act upon that knowledge for the betterment of your company. Those acts include goal setting and the strategies developed to meet those goals.

Though sometimes not as cognitive, the history of relationships sees the same thing.

✳ ✳ ✳

ANNIVERSARIES

I think it is important to celebrate successes. In marriage, it is common to celebrate anniversaries as milestones in the success of your relationship. In the same way, you will see businesses celebrate their 10th anniversary, 25th anniversary, 50th anniversary, 75th anniversary or/and 100th anniversary. Politicians will have a victory celebration when their candidate has successfully run their race in the marketplace.

On a smaller and more frequent scale, you will see Customer Appreciation days or customer loyalty gifts in the marketplace. These go a long way towards stability in your relationship.

There are numerous ways that you can celebrate milestones with your customers and show them how much you appreciate them and their loyalty to the marriage. But it's also important to celebrate within yourself. YOU have a lot to celebrate as well. In business, this often comes out in Employee Appreciation days or executive retreats and conferences. It is important to recognize where you have been and what you have done well. This inspires the company to continue with increased passion and focus.

* * *

PLANNING FOR THE FUTURE

Recognizing where you are and your end goal, it may be time to start trying to have children. Now, this depends on your goals and what you want in your marriage. In business, this might look like opening new locations or adding additional products/services to your business.

~MAINTAINING~

Some businesses are perfectly satisfied to continue in their relationship without proactively growing. Maybe the couple doesn't want to have children. They don't want to sell their home, buy a new house, and move.

And that is perfectly fine. But even in these cases, you will need to re-dedicate yourself to your efforts in maintaining who you are and your position in the marketplace. Life is constantly moving, and if you are standing still, you are going to be passed by others who are moving. So even if your goals include maintaining your positioning in the marketplace, you have to make business and communication strategies that keep up with life around you.

For some, this may include entering the world of social media or/and digital marketing because that is where the world has moved. For others, it may mean adding a drive-thru because consumers in your town aren't taking the time to eat out anymore. Maybe it means product improvement.

That leads me to another: the rise and fall of Atari[4]. Atari was the number one video gaming company in the marketplace when I was a child. They had grown in the marketplace from building some of the first coin-operated, arcade-style video gaming units to creating the best home video gaming system in the world. They called it the VCS, short for Video Computer System[tm] but it was eventually rebranded as the Atari 2600. But there was a mistake or two that happened in-between, and those mistakes, led to the video game crash of 1983 and death of Atari's positioning in the marketplace.

In an effort to keep up with demand after entering the home video game arena, Atari made a deal with Warner. Warner was a very successful entertainment company that was engaged in the production of music, film, television, and publishing. Warner saw video gaming in much the same way as they did their other enterprises. To them, Atari was like an artist on one of their record labels. Once an artist releases an album, the record label will release and promote singles off of that record for as long as they possibly can before they allow the artist to release another album. The difference here is that video gaming, Atari, was technology-based, and technology changes at a much faster rate than music.

While the label was releasing "singles for the album," or game cartridges for the Atari VCS, advances in technology were making the system obsolete. Atari wasn't allowed to explore additional systems or advances in the core gaming system because the games were still selling wildly, and if they made a newer/better system, then the investment into the VCS would seem futile or at least not "maximized" to Warner.

As the companies stood by their VCS internally, the marketing engine of Warner was running full speed, and Atari was a huge hit in the marketplace until the short-sightedness caught up with them. Marketing knew what was needed to capture the consumers' attention and sell units … and they did just that. But over time, the system couldn't deliver on what marketing was promising. The packaging was misleading. The packaging art and advertising were most always conceptual in nature, ensuring that they didn't show the limitations of the console graphically.

SUPER COOL
CONCEPTUAL
GAME BOX

ACTUAL GAME

ACTUAL GAME

SUPER COOL
CONCEPTUAL
GAME POSTER

Then, when the marketing went into really high-gear, it made that difference even more appalling. Let me explain.

Warner began using its relationships with other entertainment businesses to help sell the video games. They partnered with the Steven Spielberg's movies *E.T.* and *Raiders of the Lost Ark* through licensing the name of those brands and relating it to games for the VCS. They also licensed the number one coin-operated video game in the world – *Pac-man*.

The marketing was very high-end and promised great things for the home gaming market, but in the end, the system couldn't provide the necessary graphics and gaming experiences that the customers expected. The VCS wasn't capable of doing it. The graphics and game-play were well below par with expectations. Atari hadn't been allowed to continue innovation of the technology, and customers simply stopped being interested in video gaming. They tried to course-correct, much like the Coke story, but it was too late – the video game crash of 1983 was on them.

We will jump back into video gaming in the next chapter to continue this story, but the point here is that Atari didn't do what was necessary to maintain their position in the marketplace. In their case, this need would have included continuing to advance in technology and hardware to support the needs and desires of the ever-changing marketplace.

~Expansion ~

After some time, after the marriage has been established, many people will start to ask if the couple is going to start having children. This may have been part of the dream for the business owner from the beginning, or it may just seem like the natural progression of things for many. But if your goals include expanding your business, then after a successful year is often the best time to ask yourself about growth.

You've laid your foundation, entered the marketplace, established your positioning, and now is the time for growth. So again, we go into strategy mode. We have two goals, one is maintaining the customer base and positioning in the market, but we also want to grow in the marketplace.

Now what that looks like will, again, depend on the goals of the business. Goals lead strategy. If you are going to have children strategically, you have to plan for a smooth transition. Do you need to buy a new family car? Will you need to add a new room for the baby? Do you need to think about what school district you are going to be in?

In business, we ask "how can we improve our positioning?" What is in the overall strategy from the previous year that we couldn't afford to do because of budgetary restrictions at the time? In marriage, you might have considered living in the affluent area of town, but you couldn't afford it, so you made concessions. Now that you have a year or two under your belt, you can reinvest into your goals and finally get that home in the better neighborhood, better suited for growing your family. In business, you would reinvest those dollars profited from the previous year into those areas of marketing and operations that will begin to increase your growth in the most efficient and effective ways possible within your newer, increased budgets.

There is no resting when growing a business. Several business owners think that, after a successful year, they can simply do nothing and "live off the fat of the land." But that is never the case. You can celebrate, as I said earlier, but the work will not go away. Those profits should be reinvested into your business until you have reached your goals, or your goals change... And I believe it should all be done proactively with strategic planning.

SUCCESS
(SALE OF BUSINESS • RETIREMENT • LEGACY)

When I first create a strategy for a client, at the end of the brand development stages, there are often several strategic elements that they couldn't afford to implement at the time. So we prioritized what would be best for them based on where the company was at the time and the budgetary realities that existed. After a successful year, the first places we consider for the coming year are often those strategic elements that were left on the table initially. Maybe it was determined then that it would be recommended that the company advertise on digital radio to reach more of their potential audience, but they couldn't afford the minimum investment. So we put it off until they could grow enough to cover those costs... and now they are there.

In other circumstances, maybe costs have changed in the past year, and you can now afford to do something you didn't think possible before. Or maybe there is a new opportunity that didn't exist before. Maybe technology has advanced, and there are new possibilities available that simply didn't exist 12 – 18 months prior.

All of these elements are considered at this time, and we begin to develop a new strategy for the coming year. Also to note, a business' year doesn't necessarily mean a calendar year. In the same way that a farmer's calendar or a school calendar doesn't follow January through December, a business' calendar may not either. It simply refers to a set period of time.

The important elements in this stage are to look at your previous year, see how far you've progressed towards your goals, to celebrate what went well, analyze what worked and why, also look at what didn't work and why, and then plan for the future according to new or existing goals for the business.

To bring it back to our analogy, a couple will look at their life, their careers, their positioning, etc. and evaluate it in light of their goals before making a decision towards expanding their family. Then make the necessary plans accordingly. They may include moving to that new school district or buying that new minivan, or maybe it's taking that next trip overseas together before considering a family.

CHAPTER TEN

AVOIDING DIVORCE

I've set the next part of the Measure stage into a separate chapter to line it up with our marriage analogy. I've called it "Avoiding Divorce." In business terms, we would call it Course Correction.

If anything in the previous year did NOT go well, it is, again, important to analyze why. Don't just sweep it under the rug. Figure out what went wrong, why is your marriage off to a rocky start, and what can you do to save it? Then invest in getting back on course. If you make no changes, nothing will change. If you don't water your plant, it will surely die. A definition of insanity is to repeat the same things but expect different results.

However, it is also important to stay true to your course. Who you are and what your goals were will likely be the same as when you started. Don't give up, just course correct. A little tweak where necessary can make all the difference, and it doesn't have to have been a catastrophe in your year. Maybe a simple strategic element simply didn't turn out the way you expected... find out why and tweak it accordingly.

Life in marriage and in business is ever-changing. There are very few absolutes. Business consultants will often say, "test, test, then test again." to ensure you stay on the right path. Maintaining course towards your goal is what matters.... not blame. Mistakes happen. Misgivings happen. Errors happen. Life is fluid. Accept it. Learn from it. And move on, but don't do it again.

Keep in constant communication with your bride. Know what they need. Make concessions. Provide. And course correct when necessary to ensure you are always on the same path to strengthening your relationship and building growth.

Now, I promised to go back to video gaming. After the demise of Atari, Nintendo re-entered the home video game marketplace, but they had learned a few things from Atari's story. They brought out their gaming system, the Nintendo Entertainment System, aka NES, but then continued to reinvest and innovate their core product in addition to game development. Let's jump into their story with the Nintendo Entertainment System, NES. The NES gave way to Super Nintendo, which was succeeded by Nintendo 64, then Game Cube, then Wii, then the Nintendo Switch. This was all industry-level course correction based on the history of their predecessor. Other systems followed the same path – Playstation, PS2, PS3, PS4, etc.

They also made note to show what game play would actually look like on their cartridges. This would ensure that consumers knew what they were getting in the way of graphics.

CHAPTER ELEVEN

WHAT IF I'M ALREADY MARRIED

Ah, this can be tricky. If you are married and realize that you didn't do the homework upfront that is necessary for a successful relationship, you ignored the warning signs, or "red flags" as they are called in my house, or perhaps your spouse lied to you about who they were, and you have found yourself living with a stranger. In any case, you find yourself faced with an unpleasant choice depending on your situation and your goals. Let's explore:

* * *

GO BACK TO THE BEGINNING

Sometimes, businesses will come to me when they have taken their business as far as they can on their own and are now looking for professional help to compete better or more efficiently. It's not uncommon and is often a good thing. It usually means that the business has had some moderate success, and they simply didn't set out to professionally develop their brand from the beginning; they ran the business as far as they could on their own; and have gotten into a place where they need professionals to help take their business to the "next level".

It's a "good thing" for a couple of reasons. One, because of their moderate success to date, they should have reasonable resources to devote to professional brand development, and it will happen much faster for them from this point forward. Two, there is a good chance that there is an established consumer base that we can interview to gain initial insight from.

I also have to praise them because they took action. They were savvy enough to realize they needed brand development and are now seeking it. I've seen many business owners who are simply in denial. The sooner they recognize the need for brand development the better, but it does not come without pain, that pain is in recognizing wasted time and investment.

So there's the "bad" side: by not accomplishing brand development sooner in the company's history, there is likely going to be a rebuilding effort in several areas. I have had businesses come to me in this circumstance where they had just finished building a new website, and they will now have to rebuild an even newer one because the first one they developed was devoid of brand. Often, the things the company developed previously, outside of their brand, will need to be re-done to include their brand once they have it developed. This will position them better for success, but realizing the loss in the previous investment is often difficult to swallow. It is better for a company to have a brand, always. Anything designed without a brand will, unfortunately, need to be corrected. It's best to just accept it as lessons learned and move forward.

Then, the process is relatively the same as for companies that have started with brand development earlier in their history.

* * *

REBRANDING
"This isn't the person I thought I was marrying."

So you are already married but are running into problems. Your bride doesn't seem as happy as they once were, or you are not as satisfied in your relationship as before. During these times, we go "back to the drawing board." It's not uncommon, and, in business, we call it "rebranding."

Rebranding is like marriage counseling and involves revisiting the brand development process, this time from the company's current circumstances. In some cases, rebranding will happen after a major shift in the marketplace or as a form of major course correction for a business that has become stagnant in the marketplace.

In these cases, we will analyze the company's current situation. What does the public think about them currently? How are they positioned in the marketplace? Where are they in the competitive landscape? Has their targetable audience changed? And is their brand difference one that matters most to their target audience currently?

Then, we set our tasks on leading them through the

process based on where they are currently and what needs to be done to help them achieve their goals. Sometimes rebranding is simple and just involves some defined tasks of redefining and recommunicating who they are. Other times, it involves creating a whole new identity for the business.

Let's look at an example: "Old Spice" – This was a product line that entered the marketplace in 1937. It was marketed with a nautical theme that embraced the origins of the spice trade in colonial America. It was very successful in its day. But when it came to the new generations of the 2000s, they were losing market share, partially because the marketing was outdated and because it reminded the younger generation of their grandfather. Because they were very successful during their grandfathers' youth and brand loyalty to the product was so strong that the men continued to use it. But 70 years after launch, the company had become stagnant and out of touch with modern consumers. It was then rebranded with contemporary marketing and packaging that was more relevant to the younger generations. It embraced humor and being cheeky while utilizing viral videos and social media (more current media types), introduced new products that fit the modern male, etc. They didn't change their logo or their origins, but were revitalized by rebranding their identity in the marketplace while embracing who they were during the transition: "If your grandfather hadn't worn it, you wouldn't exist." Now, they are known for embracing manly behavior while using humor.

Another example: "Sound of Music" – Founded in 1966, the company was a retail store that sold stereo equipment. By the 1980s, the "hi-fi" market was changing, and the company was rebranded as "Best Buy" and now includes all types of home electronics technology. This was a complete rebrand as opposed to the previous.

There are several common reasons why an existing company may seek to rebrand:

- CHANGES IN OWNERSHIP – MERGER, ACQUISITION, ETC.
  Often when a company is bought, they will be rebranded with the new owners' vision.

- CHANGES IN LEADERSHIP
  Sometimes, when leadership in a company changes, the new owner will want to make their version of the company significantly different than the previous.

- REPOSITIONING IN THE MARKETPLACE – NEW TARGET
  As markets change, businesses have to change with them. If your targeted market size reduces, many companies will consider rebranding in an effort to pursue new or additional markets.

- GOING INTERNATIONAL – EXPANDING YOUR MARKET
  Making the step to go international, or global, means that there will be differences within your audience's cultures. Rebranding is often a way to define how your business will relate and communicate with a more diverse consumer base.

- Disassociation / Reputation repair
  Sometimes brands can become associated with something negative in our cultures. For example, if a crime is committed within the company, its reputation and image can be forever tainted with it. Rebranding is often a way for an existing company to step away from the public's perception or correct an internal issue.

  Other times, it could be an association that isn't relative to the business operations at all. For example, if there was a crime spree involving a certain brand of restaurants, the public may feel unsafe about dining there, even after the criminal has been caught and brought to justice. Rebranding could be a way for the company to step away from their customers' remembering the negative association.

  An example of this could be Avid Life Media. Avid Life Media is most recognized as being the owner of AshleyMadison.com. The site/business was hacked and more than 30 million customer accounts, that bought in based on anonymity and trust, were exposed. It was one of the largest security breaches in history. To save the company, they brought in new leadership and new branding as they became "Ruby Corp." Publically announcing new leadership is often a part of the relative rebranding. When coupled with a name change, it showcases a seriousness in the change to the public.

Blackwater USA, a security contractor, was in crisis after the public learned of the methods they used in Iraq and Afghanistan, which led to the deaths of civilians, and their lack of cooperation with the US Congress. The company rebranded twice before becoming Academi which created distance for them from the damage.

- NATURAL EVOLUTION

  Sometimes, it is just the natural evolutions of businesses to make changes to their communications and image. For example, Mike's Repair Shop may become Mike and Sons Repair Shop. You can also see this when companies add "and more" to their name – Bob's Books and more. This may have naturally occurred when Bob had to add movies or comics to his offerings because the demand for books in the marketplace was waning. These all represent times when rebranding could occur.

- Differentiation in the Marketplace

  Sometimes, a business will enter the marketplace and not stand out at all. This is a problem, so they need to go through a rebranding to determine how they can make a difference in the marketplace.

- Updates in the Marketplace

  A larger brand-related update in the marketplace is often referred to as a rebrand as well. This is most often when a company's appearance and operations have become antiquated, and they are doing a sizable refresh of their look and/or operations in the marketplace that is noticeable by the public.

* * *

DIVORCE AND START AGAIN

Though it isn't preferred, some marriages just don't seem to work. For one reason or another, the couple decides they cannot stay together.

Sometimes rebranding is not an option. When a company has lost its way and the owners, leadership, or employees decide to go their own way.

This happened with Atari[4]. When leadership had a disagreement with the top few game programmers, the employees left and started Activision. You remember Activision, the company that came up with Chopper Command, Pitfall, River Raid, and all the games that were so much better than what Atari was putting out. Game innovation had stopped at Atari, and innovation was something the company was built on. When the new leadership didn't want to invest in game innovation, the top designers took up the mantel but did it as their own separate company. Once the core creative element of Atari, they divorced management and the rest of the company to rebrand themselves as a new business entity.

Another example, Handy Dan Home Improvement was one of the first home improvement niche retailers.

Two in their leadership were let go – Arthur Blank and Bernie Marcus. The business owner, Sanford Sigoloff, had a personality clash when these two gentlemen which is simply to say that they had different visions. Handy Dan was a premium chain, believed in high customer service and in having very specialized areas for growing their business. Blank and Marcus wanted to make changes based on their competitive landscape and a few rogue ideas. They wanted to be the Sears and Roebuck of home-improvement. They wanted to open huge stores with no frills, huge selection, and high-grade service. They wanted to utilize volume-discounts to produce inventory turnover. They wanted to demystify home repair and educate homeowners on how they could do things themselves. But they weren't owners of Handy Dan, and after they divorced the company, Blank and Marcus went on to start Home Depot.

Home Depot has gone on to include an empire of more than 2300 locations in North America and spawned an industry of big-box retailers.

CHAPTER TWELVE

Conclusion

So I guess to sum everything up, I would say that we've explored and explained many ways how marriage and business are alike in more ways than most people think.

- Marriage is a conceptual construct in the same way that Business is.

- Both take undying commitment.

- Both take an investment in time and money.

- Both take planning.

- Communication is key in both areas.

- Both start with a wink and a nod then move towards more meaningful, loyal relationships.

- Both are comprised of multiple phases and stages.

- They both have right and wrong ways to accomplish them... and a few in between as well.

So, Business Owners and Executive Professionals, I hope that this book makes the complications, ups and downs, and the journey through the world of business more relatable and understandable for you.

The keys to business lie in understanding the path, knowing the challenges, and having the drive necessary to see things through to success. May God bless you in your journey.

EPILOGUE

The Finance | The Commitment

So, you've decided you want to get married - you want to run your own business - to be in charge of your "destiny." Now you know what you are in for. It has its rewards, but it's a journey. I always believe that there is power, wisdom, and credibility in knowledge.

So now you know, what you are going to do with that knowledge? Now is the time where you "buck up or shut up." It's where you "put your money where your mouth is." And it's "where the rubber meets the road." But it's also a crossroads where you have to make a decision. Do you build or buy? I find that many of life's decisions can be boiled down to this choice: **Build vs Buy**.

* * *

BUILD

By *BUILD*, I am not referring to your building. I am referring to DIY or doing-it-yourself. As a younger, early business owner, we have a tendency to wear many hats and to try and accomplish as much as we can on our own. Usually, this is in direct juxtaposition to available financial resources.

If you do it yourself, there are some benefits. You will normally invest less financially upfront because you are investing more of your own time.

- Time to learn and develop the skills necessary to accomplish the tasks.

- Time spent actually accomplishing said tasks.

This is true with any task, not just the ones

mentioned in this book. But normally, the more you take on your shoulders, the more stress will be introduced into your life as well.

DIY
- MORE TIME INVESTED
- LESS MONEY INVESTED
- DEVELOP EXPERTISE
- MORE STRESS

* * *

BUY

By saying *BUY*, I am not referring to buying your own business as opposed to launching your own. I am really talking about outsourcing or hiring expertise and labor.

- Buying or paying for someone else to accomplish certain tasks for you either because it will save you time or because they are simply better educated, experienced, or prepared to complete those tasks.

If you hire a third party or partner with an

organization or individual for certain specialized tasks, you will invest more financially, but it will also free up your own time, allowing you to focus more on your core business and further developing THOSE skills.

For some, this brings less worry, and therefore, less stress. But it is different for each person according to their own situations and their own skill sets.

OUTSOURCED
- LESS TIME INVESTED
- MORE MONEY INVESTED
- HIRED EXPERTISE
- LESS STRESS

THE CHOICE

This really is one of the most important choices that you will make in many areas of your life, not just business. For example, I know how to change the oil in my car... but I'm not going to do it because I feel like my time is better spent doing other things - whether that means working or spending time with family. So it's not about whether I have the ability to do it, in this case.

At one time in the agency's history, I built all of our creative department's computers myself because I knew how to do it, it was more cost-effective for me to do so, and my life allowed for me to have the time to do it. However, as we grew, our business became busier, and the cost of computers came down, I decided that it was worth it to have our computers built by a service instead of my taking the time to do it myself. In this case, it was a question of time and efficiency.

Pride, emotion, and being frugal can often get in the way of what is best for your business. Those areas of often red flags in business. But only you know what is going to be best in the present situation. These types of decisions fall on you as the owner or leader of your business.

I am a business owner, and sometimes I will "do it myself" as opposed to having another complete the task for various reasons.

- Because I find it would take more time to accomplish the tasks to my satisfaction when considering that I might have a higher skill level in accomplishing it.

In this case, it's more about how quickly we can get

the job accomplished well.

Considering is a key word here. You have to take the time to be honest with yourself and consider your assets, your skills, your experiences, your time, and your standards before making the decision - whatever that decision may be regarding. As the business owner, I am in charge of these decisions for my company. I am responsible for maintaining efficiency when it comes to costs vs. time. And sometimes, it more valuable to the company for me to spend my own time in other areas.

At the same time, you don't want to allow laziness or the prospect of being financially unwise to be a factor either. Just because I don't want to do laundry doesn't mean I'm going to have a service dry clean all my clothes. Contrarily, in this same example, if I am working 18 hours a day doing my core business tasks, and I can't seem to find time to get my laundry done, I may decide that it is more cost-effective for me to keep working and then to pay for the service to accomplish the tasks. And again, if I have a stain on my sport-coat that I don't possess the skills to remove, I'm also not going to spend my time trying to do it myself and risk ruining my blazer. It's better to let a professional do it correctly and efficiently the first time.

Time:

- How much time do I have available myself/internally?

- How much quicker can I accomplish this if I do it myself?

- How much time will it save me to delegate/outsource?

- Will it take longer for me to complete the tasks myself?

Money:

- How much capital do I have?

- How much money am I making right now doing my core business tasks?

- How much capital would I save?

- How much will it cost me if I stop what I am doing to accomplish these other tasks?

Skill:

- How much do I know about accomplishing this task from my own experience?

- Will I be better at accomplishing the task than someone else?

- Would my time be better spent investing in myself or my core skills?

- How much time will it take me to learn what I need to know to accomplish the task to my satisfaction?

- Would a hired specialist be better at accomplishing the task than me?

- Would learning this skill benefit me in enough time to be of value to the company?

Quality:

- In the end, will the results be better if I do it?

- Can I make it appear as if a professional has done it?

- In the end, will the results be better if I hired someone to do it?

- Will it make the company look unprofessional or amateur?

There are many factors that go into decisions. That's why you, the boss, are responsible to make them. You have to weigh the choice. It comes with the territory of responsibility.

* * *

THE DECISION

So every situation has a different approach to the Build vs Buy decision. The decision will not be the same in all situations. There isn't a golden rule that trumps in every case. I believe that importance should be placed on:

- Being Aware
- Being Knowledgeable
- Being Truthful
- Being Considerate
- Being Wise

I'll leave you with a little graphic that I find both humorous and true.

ENDNOTES

[1] SCORE is a non-profit resource partner from the *U.S. Small Business Administration (SBA)* that acts as the nation's largest network of volunteer, expert business mentors.

[2] A *destination restaurant* is a restaurant, sometimes themed, that has a strong enough appeal to draw customers outside of its community.

[3] It is interesting to note that in 2019, there was a brief resurgence of "New Coke" due to the launch of the 3rd season of the *Stranger Things* television program. In a way, this is similar to how a married couple might look back on their story and laugh at a past transgression in their lives.

[4] To further explore the rise and fall of Atari, go to *StraightShot.net* to find a podcast episode of the same name. It is also available in the *Straight Shot Marketing Podcast* app in your smartphone's app store, on the *Straight Shot Marketing Podcast* YouTube Channel, or wherever you listen to podcasts.

KEYWORD & TOPICAL INDEX

CITATIONS

Page 29 – McKenna, Regis. *Marketing Is Everything*. Harvard Business Review, 1991

Page 77 – Star Wars Toys Don't Sell - Bolshevik Marketing and Marketing in Reverse, David Stewart, 29 Jan. 2018, 15:10, https://youtu.be/be4VNXKVKUA

"Bolshevik Marketing" - The Rhetoric of Ideas, David Stewart, 4 Feb. 2018, https://youtu.be/8Zd6ljuRikY

Pages 35-39, 41-48 – "Hitch." Columbia Pictures, 2005.

Page 78 – "Big." 20th Century Fox, 1998.

Page 60 – "The Godfather." Paramount Pictures, 1972

Page 118, 119 – "Raiders Of The Lost Ark." Paramount Pictures, 1981

Page 119 – "E.T., the Extra-Terrestrial." Universal Pictures, 1982

Pages 114-120, 127-128, 139, 153 – "Easy to Learn, Hard to Master: The Fate of Atari." Journeyman Pictures, 2017

Pages 84, 106-107, 109-110 – "Trouble At The Top: The People vs Coke." BBC, 2003

Pages 84, 106-107, 109-110 – "Empires of Industry – Cola Wars." A&E Home Video, 2006

Page 134 – Best Buy. International Directory of Company Histories, Vol.63. St. James Press, 2004

Page 139-140 – Sellers, Patricia. *Home Depot: Sigoloff's unsung legacy*. Fortune, 2011

Page 139-140 – Loeb, Walter. *The Story Of Ken Langone, The Visionary Behind Home Depot*. Forbes, 2018

Page 139-140 – *Bernie Marcus & Arthur Blank*. Entreprenuer, 2008

Page 95 – Bellini, Jarrett. *The No. 1 thing to consider before opening a restaurant*. CNBC, 2016, Mar 15

Pages 133-134 – Borisov, Sergey. *The Beginning of a Legend: Early American Old Spice*. Fragrantica.com, 2019, May 24

Pages 133-134 – Girvin, Tim. *Old Spice: Scent, Brandstory, Social Media: Legacies and Innovation*. Girvin.com, 2010, Sept 17

Pages 133-134 – *History of Old Spice*. Proctor & Gamble, 2019

Page 134 – Vasilogambros, Matt. *Rebranding Infidelity*. The Atlantic, 2016, July 12

Page 132-134 – Duckler, Mitch. *Rebranding: More Than Just A Name Change.* Full Surge, 2016, Aug 19

ACKNOWLEDGMENTS

I have been a key-note speaker, business coach, and marketing professional for years, so I am familiar with writing and sharing with others. But one thing I've realized that was unexpected was the distinct difference between copywriting and long-form writing. With copywriting, the goal is to write as efficiently and succinctly as possible – saying as much as you can in as few words as possible. Long-form writing is basically the opposite, but I hope you found this work helpful.

I'd like to take a moment to thank my wife for pushing me to start and complete the book and also for her graphic design skills in pulling the book together. She and my childhood friend, Leverett Butts, author of the Guns of the Waste Land series, have been very instrumental in helping me through reviewing the content and being my first two readers while in draft mode. Your input and feedback have been most valuable.

I also want to thank my daughter, Kaetlyn Bennett, for lending a hand as the final proofing of the texts. Yea English!

I'd also like to thank all the men and women I have worked with during my career that led through this journey that is marketing. I've learned so much from those around me over the years.

Thank you to all the businesses that I have studied over my career. The availability of your stories has been of great value to me.

I'd also like to thank my friends in SCORE, the SBA, the SBDC, and the Chambers I have worked with over the years. This opportunity is a direct line from your acts of faith in me.

ABOUT THE AUTHOR

B. Zachary Bennett, the principal behind *Reformation Productions*, a full-service marketing agency located in Atlanta, Georgia, comes with a 20+ year career in marketing and advertising, working to grow major companies like *Bank of America, The Limited, Vectren Corporation, TruGreen-ChemLawn, Dick's Sporting Goods, Lowe's Home Improvement, Campbell's Foods, Gwinnett Medical Center, Victoria's Secret, St. Vincent's Medical Center, Home Depot, BP, NAPA AutoParts, NAPA AutoCare,* and more.

Since starting his own boutique agency and providing his marketing expertise and skills to local and regional clients, he has dedicated his time and efforts to the pursuit of helping educate business professionals on the ways that the marketing process has been perfected by Fortune 500 companies, bringing his experience to local and regional companies in ways that they can afford.

Zachary is often asked to be a keynote or guest speaker at industry conferences, Chambers of Commerce, networking groups, business conferences, and more. He is a frequent speaker for the SBDC, SCORE, SBA, and the Gwinnett Chamber.

He is also available for one-on-one marketing consultation, provides outsourced and interim CMO services, and leads custom workshops and seminars.

Reformation Productions is dedicated to helping companies market their businesses in the most effective and efficient ways possible with a process used by Fortune 500 companies called Straight Line Marketing. Find out more about the agency at ReformationProductions. com or call 678.825.8086.

www.BZacharyBennett.com

Thanks for reading!
*Please add a short review on **Amazon***
and let me know what you thought!

It is always great to hear your thoughts and experiences from reading the book.

Please visit our website at www.BZacharyBennett.com and let us know you've left a review on Amazon. It will help us a lot, and we'd love to say thank you.

You can also connect with the Married To Marketing community on Facebook.com/groups/marriedtomarketing

We are going to have a giveaway contest! Please take a photo of yourself with the book, post it on social media with the hashtag #MarriedToMarketing, and tag B. Zachary Bennett on facebook or/and instagram.

FB.com/BZacharyBennett
Instagram.com/bzacharybennett

Also from
B. Zachary Bennett

MARRIED TO MARKETING WORKBOOK

For business owners, entrepreneurs, and other professionals that are looking for a hands-on, companion piece to MARRIED TO MARKETING by B. Zachary Bennett, this workbook is designed to help develop a very personal, in-depth understanding of the marketing process and the relative business commitment as it applies to your specific business. This is the same workbook that Mr. Bennett uses with his one-on-one, business-coaching clients in leading them through developing their brand, strategy, and communication tools.

As a supplemental resource, this workbook walks you through the processes and questions shared in M2M in a way that is specific for you and your own business.

- Guided Processes
- Expanded Discussion
- Checklists
- Schedules
- Results Tracking

- Thought Provoking Questions
- Brand Development
- Strategic Planning
- Message Development
- And Much More...

www.ingramcontent.com/pod-product-compliance
Lightning Source LLC
Chambersburg PA
CBHW021410210526
45463CB00001B/300